Bronx Local

Poems by
Patrick Hammer, Jr.

NoNet Press
New York City

Bronx Local

First North American Publication 2014

Copyright © 2014 Patrick Hammer, Jr.

Printed in the U.S.A.
Cover photo and author photo from the author's collection.

And the thoughts of youth are long, long thoughts.

Longfellow

As Carrie Watts longs for Bountiful; Charles Ryder for Brideshead; Proust for Combray; Dylan Thomas for Swansea; Wordsworth for The Lakes, I dedicate this collection of memories to my sisters, Kathy and Patsy, and to my brother, Hank, hoping they, too, find something of their lost selves here.

TABLE OF CONTENTS

ARRIVAL

Off the Deegan, descending on Fordham
down down to Sedgwick
down to University
over Jerome, over Creston
over the Concourse
back back to Valentine
over Marion – Decatur Decatur
I have arrived.

Back back over 50 40 30...
No, I am 10. It's 1966 thereabouts
here at the corner
of Decatur and Fordham.
CYpress5- I would have called.
Housed in this dream
in the shadow of the el
the narrow room of these lines
carry bigger rooms, bigger lives
to the child that I was, the I
that was him.

Back back to summers
of Botanical color, the Zoo
of striped zebras, tigers.
A world still watching black and white.
Back back to these sultry Bronx streets.

Up up to the third floor.
Knock knock knocking to be let in.
Nana, Nana, it can't be over,
the he that is I is saying.
Nana, Nana, open up, let me in.

1

FLAT

Nana's bathroom smells of Dove soap.
The frosted window, above the cast-
iron, claw-footed tub, open an inch.
Stale back-alley-air, muffled, mysterious,
filled with mechanical sounds, drifts in.
The kitchen has treasures to explore:
Nana's red formica table has a metal
ring underneath; I pull it often,
hoping a hidden chamber will open.
Here's the sealed-off dumbwaiter
forbidden as a pharaoh's tomb.
Here are the red and white dishes
with the Chinese patterns of foot-
bridges and willows that I want
to cross and climb. Here the red
rotary phone on the wall,
the Kelvinator fridge with the beige
radio atop that's the size of a loaf,
that takes minutes to warm up
and then blasts the news. Here's
the double sink, the stove, the spot
where Nana always seems to be.
Down this railroad flat, on the right,
the living room bathed in mellow
torch lamp light. A fake log-burning
fire crackles in a fake grate.
The mantle of the fireplace held up
by two hard-working grimacing
gargoyles. Here among the bric-a-brac
framed school photos of me collared,
dress-shirted, blue-suited, in a butterfly

2

tie, a paisley clip-on. Me in all white,
hands in prayer, holding a missal, rosary,
making my first Communion. Completing
the room the Grundig Console radio
and turntable that Nana says came from
a place called Radio Row.
Out of this room, I turn right again,
walk along the white-and-gold speckled
wall, into my grandparents' room,
its two large windows looking out
east to the tower of Fordham's
Keating Hall. Here more of Nana's
treasures: white bedspread with floral
brocade, bottles of Blue Grass, her
silver comb and brush set, the black-
lacquered, Mother of Pearl inlaid,
multi-tiered Japanese jewelry box –
all displayed on her vanity mirror.
My final destination: the spare room,
back room, my room, this room
straight through Nana's room, full
of armoires, hat boxes, shoe racks,
clothes from another season in opaque
plastic bags. I stand at the single
small window, listening to night now,
after my journey here, to other
adventurers in lawn chairs three
floors below, in a circle, telling non-
suburban tales, their laughter drifting up
to me from this building's front stoop.

NANA

Nana stands before me
wearing her low-cut floral housedress,
deep pockets full of butterscotch drops,
bobby pins, her change purse
with the price of an ice cream
when the bells of the truck ring out.
All these dollars smell like Nana.
Above her bifocals, hair dyed ash blonde,
under a neat net. Thick-armed,
ample-bosomed, deep cleavage as if
she has a second bottom.

She laughs and her dentures jiggle.
She speaks a honey-sweet brogue.
The nails of her thick fingers polished
deep red like the Irish blood we share.
All day she wears her soft, open-toed
slippers, cushioning her row of corns.

She is pints of French Vanilla from the H.
She is candied orange slices from the 5 & 10.
She is strong tea, buttered toast,
at noon and night.
She is Pepsodent tooth powder and cubes
of bluing agent side by side on the sink.
She is stew meat from her favorite butcher.
She is bus routes to Throggs Neck, Tremont,
Pelham Bay – to call on friends from Tour,
her Limerick village back home.

NEIGHBORS

All these Irish names, neat and orderly,
down the line on these vestibule buzzers,
on mailboxes in the shadowy alcove, under
the stairs, beyond the recessed marble
front hall bench. One name:
Patrick Fitzpatrick, makes me laugh.

Up we climb, Nana and I, to the third floor,
never the full five flights; there is drama
enough this far.

Mrs. Sharky's door always open a crack;
low, moaning sounds drift out.
It's the drink, Nana whispers.
God bless the mark.

Mrs. Malzar, always behind a closed door,
sneezes all day, loud and long, like an alarm,
as if she likes to play with pepper.

Mrs. Kelly, I've been told, has a spanking
machine for all bad girls and boys.
When I've seen her in Nana's church, sitting
right behind me, I always face forward
and turn to stone.

RYANS

Nana and I go out and call on the Ryans.
Lanky-tall, old, always on the street
in front of the building, in his worn
everyday suit, Irish cap, Mr. Ryan smokes
his pipe, holding court. He takes us –
back alley – through the dark passage
to their rear apartment, up a rickety
flight of wooden steps.

Mrs. Ryan, ancient to me, gaunt, white-
haired, wire rimmed glasses, always a wide,
toothy smile when she sees me. Nana, who's
washed their curtains, on a ladder now,
hanging and straightening out their lace.

Afterwards we four have tea, sip
slowly, savor the soda bread, despite
the heat, that Nana has baked.
Mr. Ryan silent as he eats. I'm learning
another lesson this late afternoon.

Walking home, I ask Nana why
she takes care of them. *Whist,* she says,
they remind me of my parents,
the creatures. Sure, they need
a bit of help.

WILLIE

Hello, Jersey! How are you, Jersey?
How did you get here? Did you fly in
by helicopter, Jersey?
It's an early lesson in humor from Willie,
Nana's German butcher, a dead ringer
for Don Ameche, but I'm not laughing.

We're in Willie's shop on Webster,
the only place Nana buys her meat.
Young, silent, but I take everything in.
Not certain if this is mockery, I have
no words, no developed sense of humor,
no magical helicopter.

Nana answers for me: *His father drove him*
in from Paramus. Embarrassed,
I kick the sawdust under my feet.
Meats hang on hooks on the wall
behind Willie.
He reaches over the counter,
hands me a morsel
of cheese. Suddenly, I find my voice:
No, no, I came in by car! Willie smiles.
Nana smiles, goes on with her order.

I wonder what I'd say to Willie
if I met him on the street, away from
his scales, slicers, and grinder.
What small talk would we make on Fordham
if I saw him out of his blood-stained
white smock.

REWARD

A perfect day for bananafish, perfect
for Salinger, even though I've never heard
of The New Yorker or Harper's, perfect
for reading this white-covered, nine-story
collection that's had a life of its own
before me.

I'm sitting in Nana's living room,
in the corner, in the ample, gold-upholstered,
tasseled chair by the window. Muggy-warm,
she's opened it. A slight breeze ripples
through the sheer lace curtain. I peer out
to the back alley of her building, watch dark
shafts of light descending, smell stale air steal
through this concrete-grit and brick corridor.
I hear the muted sounds from Marion Avenue,
a block above, from Fordham, a block south.

I turn away from lines heavy with wash,
strung across this mysterious space,
listen to Nana who's come into the room.
*Be a good lad. Read a few more pages,
the way we'll go shopping soon.*
It's a bribe. I've been promised
a bottle of Sun-Up cologne that I've wanted.
A reward for reading. Each day that I'm here
there'll be small treats. *You'll be smart and
land a good job.*

I return to Esme, to Uncle Wiggily,
to the Laughing Man. I meet
Boo Boo Tannenbaum
down at the dinghy. Don't know what to make
of her; I'm only 10. Nana, I'm reading the diary
of Theodore McArdle. Not sure that I should.
Nana, I'm learning about the Glass Family,
Presbyterians, the Queen Mary, suicides
when there's so much living yet to do.

Nana, I'm learning to like this reading – bribes
and jobs aside – simply for the sport.

FORDHAM

All rails and roads and cabs and cars,
all white-gloved, patent-leathered, floral-
hatted, women walking; all business-suited,
Florsheim-footed working men; all movement
high speed, despite muggy heat, here in
the center of my young universe. All life
pulsing like blood coursing, quicker than
the nearby Bronx River. Quicker than what
Nana and I, in a day, can cover.

Nana quizzes me on my multiplication tables.
We walk the green-lush of Bronx Park; 10x2
on Daffodil Hill, searching for long-fallen
petals, and other botanicals.
4x11 as we steal uncaged,
quiet afternoons at the zoo. After this flora,
fauna, a visit to Sear's on Webster.

Up Fordham to Gorman's long counter open
to the street, for my treat: a taut-skinned,
crunchy frank, washed down with grape soda
in a white-coned brown plastic cup. On to
Krum's, Sutter's, Zaro's for candies, cakes.
Jahn's for the Kitchen Sink.

Resting now, digesting, in Banana Park, this
island strip in the middle of traffic flow. Down-
hill to Scratch Park, on Webster again, dozing
in park-bench-shade, the whoosh of New York
Central behind us, watching bettors pencil in
their horses on bits of paper. I sip water
from a granite fountain that looks like a linga.

Nana, Nana, back up to Jerome to defend
our castle: the Kingsbridge Armory.
Nana, on to Alexander's on the Concourse
to take that bastion of fashion.
Inside the store I hear pinging
above me like a xylophone ringing a secret
message: How marvelous Fordham Road
for shoppers, for explorers,
for Nana, for me.

MARKETING

Nana and I market at the A & P on Webster.
I glide the cart slowly down each narrow aisle.
Nana fills it. No list, knows what she wants
by heart.

Gold bricks of Ann Page butter, buttermilk,
whole milk, white bread, boxes of raisins, tea,
bags of apples, potatoes, flour, jars of jelly,
jam, eggs, turnip heads, bulky rhubarb
all falling into order.

I will be helping Nana bake pies, soda bread
with caraway; carried away, white dusty
powder will flurry the kitchen this July.
She will knead and I will help her.
Lost in reverie, we move
to the front check-out counter.

A reckless young woman cuts into our line,
hits our cart, bumps into Nana.
I look for Nana's signal, ready to rage.
She doesn't turn to me, only smiles
at the woman, as if nothing has happened.

The woman pays and is gone.
Kindness, with no words spoken,
my greatest sustenance today.

KENYA

Out of the confines of staid suburbia,
into the wondrous wilds of the city,
I come with books from Paramus Library,
but not enough to last the summer.
And so I read, for a second time,
BORN FREE: A LIONESS OF TWO WORLDS.

Nana wants to grow my vocabulary to get
ahead; I only want to read these cool
mornings, this sultry summer, with Elsa,
close the cover, roam free. Nana, I can't
help it, can't be chained. Imagination is
a greater plain to roam, to thrive in,
than just a penned-in patch of green
called money from some occupation.
You job around the apartment, base camp.
Nana, you don't know I've gone to Kenya,
poised, leonine-like, in your golden chair,
ready to take up the adventure with Joy
and George and Elsa.

Elsa's devotion to these two a tribute
to her rearing, as I'm devoted to you.
I dream in this Bronx den, your living room,
that I'm also of two worlds. Like Elsa,
I'd leave my spoor, seek the wild
city, over everything, all my life.
I feel this morning, so early in summer,
so early in my guarded life, safe
as if in a pride of lions, safe to paw
and explore. Like the Adamsons
finally releasing their lioness, Nana
one day you'll have to release me, too.

WOOLWORTH'S

We get lost
in Woolworth's
Nana and I
down the long
narrow aisles
she's looking for
pin cushions
hair pins   corn
pads for her feet
I yearn for books
for paper   pens
to help me record
our story
summer afternoons
such as this
we wander through
buttons   notions
bottles   butter dishes
needles and thread
artificial flowers
and the like

Outside again
breathing fresh air
Nana buys me
a science workbook
from a nun
cocooned in black
selling on the street
filled with riddles
and questions
to be solved

QUEST

At night Fordham takes on
another air. The moon rises.
I become Jonny Quest of The Bronx.

Nana has a mission for me,
says I'm old enough, safe enough,
know my way around.

She sends me out for provisions
from the deli a block away on Webster,
her order in my pocket.

I take a short cut, thinking it's
a secret: the creepy tunnel connecting
through a building on Decatur.

I hand my contact at the counter
my Commander's coded message: Virginia
ham, elbow, rye, grape soda, Wise chips.

Food dispatched, Nana has new
instructions: climb up Fordham to Creston,
seek out Con, her brother.

Under cover of darkness
I leave again, carrying an urgent
directive: Come Eat Now!

JIMMY

How are you? I'm having a great summer.
Hello to everybody on Lockwood Drive.
I'm reading my book, it's a mystery:
THE HAPPY HOLLISTERS ON A RIVER TRIP.
I crossed a river too, the Hudson,
to reach this place and my grandmother.

After bacon and sausages from the butcher,
Nana makes me take a morning bath.
I hate it, hurry back to my friends
in the book: Peter, Pam, Ricky, Holly
and Sue. They're from Pine Lake
in Shoreham. I don't know where that is
but I know it's not New Jersey.

They're all great navigators, problem
solvers like my Nana here in this foreign
land called The Bronx. Nana and I
walk these hot city streets where
everyone looks as if they're filled
with stories. I pretend to look
for the Trading Post from the book.
Laughing, Nana holds my hand, doesn't let go.

*Is there any other creature you want
us to look for?* I seem to hear Rick say.
Yes, I think, help me to find meaning
in the strange creature that I am becoming,
formed by the hand that holds me.

Yes, Jim, that's the real mystery
as we explore Marion, Valentine,
Webster, Jerome. These unrushed days
flow without end, Shoreham to Fordham.
Time enough to wander; Nana and I both
play narrator. All days end happy here
on Decatur Avenue like Jerry West's
books by the last page.

MISSAL

Nana gives me a Daily Missal,
St. Joseph's, Pre-Vatican II, some of it
in Latin, leathered cover, gold-edged pages,
illustrated with Saints, a book of Devotions,
instructions for the Roman Mass,
and I use it.

We walk up Fordham to Our Lady
of Mercy on Marion, Nana's home parish,
the church I was baptized in at 3 weeks.
We visit both Upper and Lower
Sanctuaries, pray; I leaf the pages
of my missal, enter the box, make Confession.

We take the bus to Pelham, a pilgrimage
seeking Indulgences, stop on Mace Avenue,
at St. Lucy's Church, light candles, marking
my successful eye operation at 2 years.
Holy Lucy, Patroness of Eyes, we kneel to you.
Nana fingers her stark wooden black beads.

I have my own portal, this missal, thumbing
the index for the right Intention, thanking
Lucy, Blessed Mary, my Grandmother
for saving my sight, recall hearing Nana
kissed the palms of my eye surgeon
at Columbia Presbyterian, saying:
God Bless, God Bless your hands.

VAMPIRES

My grandmother loves vampires.
It's not all Gunsmoke and Lawrence Welk,
not all Merv Griffin and Carol Burnett.
We're in luck: it's Vampire Week
on late night TV: Mark Of The Vampire,
The Return Of The Vampire, The Return
Of Dracula. We sit on the coffin-length
couch, in the dim living room, viewing
the undead on the box. She has a crush
on Lugosi, curls her hair around her finger,
bobby pins it down for the night.
We eat ice cream out of pint containers.
Up past midnight, watching demons stalk
the black and white landscapes of these
B movies. So much evil at stake; so much
horror to enjoy.

And tomorrow, for certain, in late afternoon,
as dusk approaches, we'll watch
Barnabas Collins on Dark Shadows,
the cursed, guilt-ridden
resident vampire of Collinsport, Maine,
moving through Collinwood with Wolf's Head
cane, Inverness cape, bloody fangs to boot.
Nana loves her supernatural morality plays
acted out in newfangled color...and so do I.

NOIR

Nana loves her stars.
She introduces me to Joan Bennett's
Secret Beyond The Door, to Clifton Webb
and Dana Andrews both falling
for the glamour of Laura, to Kim
and Jimmy in Hitch's Vertigo,
to Barbara Stanwyck's double crossing
Double Indemnity. I'm learning
the dark world of Noir without knowing
the word. I meet Ray Milland wooing
Stella By Starlight in a ghostly world
of The Uninvited. We're at home
watching on Nana's new console TV:
the 4:30 Movie, Million Dollar Movie,
later The Late Show film.

Nana loves going out to her matinees, too.
After lunch we race to make the film.
I imagine we're in a comedy: this rushing
to hide away all afternoon from the sun,
leaving sidewalk grit and the din
of Fordham traffic. We take in all
the latest features in the dark air
conditioned air. I'm summer schooling
in a visual language of film: long shots,
close-ups, montages, pans. Nana loves
the Valentine, the RKO Fordham, the Fox.
But best of all, Loew's Paradise on the hill.

PARADISE

Paradise on the Grand Concourse –
you movie palace like a museum.
I marvel, listen to another boy,
a uniformed, capped usher, who speaks
to Nana and me. Your Depression Deco
exterior gives way to a Baroque
I've never seen: goldfish in your
marble fountain, bronze doors
that open to a lush, plush lobby.
The usher calls it Atmospheric.
Nana indulges me – we promenade
up and down your Grand Stair.
Birds and buds and vines,
statues and murals and cypress trees,
chandeliers and oil paintings –
one of an Empress called Antoinette –
all this I've never seen before.

And in the balcony – dumbstruck.
We sit under the ceiling: a dark blue
night sky. This summer afternoon stars
blink as clouds pass by. Here I meet
Milland again, and Oliver and Jenny,
in a sad Love Story. Here I sit
with Nana. We sing, despite the Nazis,
with von Trapps to The Sound Of Music.
O Paradise, Paradise, what pleasure.

AVIATOR

It is time to speak of Pop,
on the periphery all the days of these
summers, all day at work, downtown
on Liberty, an 'indoor aviator' flying
his riders to their different floors.

Jolly-stout, ruddy, his full head of wispy
brown-grey curls bounce as he throws
his head back to laugh, and he laughs often
at his own jokes, at himself.

Pop who plays his fiddle in the back room,
out of the way, who plays his reel to reels
of Paddy Noonan on the accordion, who plays
LPs of the McCusker Brothers Ceili Band
on his old Victrola, who spends nights
away from the TV writing lengthy
letters to his Irish friends back home,
who tells the same long-winded tall tales
till Nana throws him the eye, who loves
his Daily News and says he'd walk all the way
to South Ferry for a copy, who turns in
early after his extensive evening prayers.

For him I am in my usual look-out position,
at their bedroom window this early evening,
leaning out, my elbows on a pillow, protection
from the rough concrete sill. I crane my head
to the right, watch for Pop's familiar canter,
turning the corner off Fordham onto Decatur.
I shout to Nana in the kitchen:
He's coming, he's coming!

And so she lights the fire under the spuds,
peeled and quartered, waiting
to boil in the pot on the stove.
Soon we three will smother them
with butter, eat them with a chop and veg,
wash it all down, as we do every night,
with a nice cuppa.

CHARIOT

It's my first time. It's an adventure.
A dark, sultry night on Fordham.
We're waiting at the corner of Decatur,
under the globes of the pawnbroker's shop,
not our usual stop for bus or train.
Nana lifts her hand, hails a taxi.
One pulls up. We get in.
All leathery, cushiony, ample. So new
to me, so privileged, so special.

We travel uphill to Kingsbridge,
to visit Nana's distant cousin, Molly.
I imagine this driver in the front
our chauffeur, this cab for our own
decadent comfort alone.
I'm oblivious to the ticking meter.

Later I sit in Molly's flat,
in the living room, while she and Nana
drink tea in the kitchen. I turn
the knob of Molly's Admiral, nothing
on TV holds my attention.
Nana checks on me, knows what
I'm thinking, says softly:
Be patient, let ye, you'll ride again.
It's all I can think of – another procession
home in our very own yellow chariot.

BANISHMENT

Each summer comes to an end
with the start of that pit-of-the-stomach
ache, leaving The Bronx for another year.
Busy now buying my uniform and supplies.
Busy regulating my bedtime hour.

There'll be Holiday visits, unexpected
drop-ins, but none of this counts.
There'll even be a weekend over
for Kathy and Patsy, who've heard
the summer fun I've had. They'll cry
at Nana's late in the night, frightened
by city sounds, roaches, real or imagined,
moving across their sheets.

It's the banishment of my homesick sisters,
but not of me. And I'm glad, planning
another sojourn. Nana, Nana, surely
we'll have other Bronx summers.

Patrick Hammer has worked as an optical assistant, library page, market researcher, U. S. census taker, telephone operator, bank clerk, bookseller, and in newspaper advertising. On the poetry scene since the mid-70s, publishing widely in small literary magazines, **Bronx Local** is his eighth chapbook. He has been a member of the Bergen Poets in northern New Jersey; Workshop Leader for the Main Street Poets and Writers in his town of Fort Lee; Co-Leader for the Wild Angels Writers Group at the Cathedral of St. John the Divine; and currently is a member of the Parkside Poets and Riverside Poets, both of Manhattan. He is a Lay Episcopal Brother in the Order of Urban Missioners.

Also available on Amazon from NoNet Press:

Fairyland Mail by Marge Hauser

Flow Of Hope by Penelope Maguffin

89002664R00020

Made in the USA
Lexington, KY
21 May 2018